Girl in a Fix

Quick Beauty Solutions

(and why they work)

Somer Flaherty and Jen Kollmer

Illustrated by Ali Douglass

ZEST BOOKS

First published in 2007 by
Zest Books, an imprint of Orange Avenue Publishing
35 Stillman Street, Suite 121, San Francisco, CA 94107
www.zestbooks.net

Created and produced by Zest Books, San Francisco, CA
© 2007 by Orange Avenue Publishing LLC
Illustrations © 2007 by Ali Douglass

Text set in Hoefler Text; title text set in Retrofit; accent text set in Rockwell

Library of Congress Control Number: 2007925700
ISBN-13: 978-0-9772660-2-9
ISBN-10: 0-9772660-2-8

CREDITS
EDITORIAL DIRECTOR: Karen Macklin
CREATIVE DIRECTOR: Hallie Warshaw
WRITERS: Somer Flaherty and Jen Kollmer
EDITOR: Karen Macklin
ILLUSTRATOR: Ali Douglass
GRAPHIC DESIGNER: Cari McLaughlin
PRODUCTION ARTIST: Cari McLaughlin

Printed in China.
First printing, 2007
10 9 8 7 6 5 4 3 2 1

Every effort has been made to ensure that the information presented is accurate. Readers are strongly advised to read product labels, follow manufacturers' instructions, and heed warnings. The publisher disclaims any liability for injuries, losses, untoward results, or any other damages that may result from the use of the information in this book.

Everyone has disastrous beauty days.

You know, those days when your friend gets bubble gum in your hair, or the most heinous zit takes over your forehead, or you wear those new sandals just when your feet start emitting some strange new odor. Sometimes it feels like the glamour stars have completely lined up against you.

This is exactly the moment that you have to remember the true secret of beauty. No, it's not luck or genetics. It's **resourcefulness and smarts**.

A girl who uses her brain and flashes a great smile is twice as fabulous as a girl who just flashes a great smile. That's where *Girl in a Fix* comes in. In this book, you'll find an arsenal of solutions for a girl's most common

beauty problems, from typical hair and skin issues to less talked about things like new hickeys and icky dandruff. And—for the clever, curious type—you'll also learn why these solutions work. Did you know that avocados can patch up split ends? Or that peaches are good for your skin because they contain alpha hydroxy acids? We've done all the research for you, so you'll never again have to think, "I should rub tomatoes on my face *why?*"

Including away-from-home remedies, and creative advice for problems that need extra quick attention,

Girl in a Fix is the essential beauty manual for all girls who like to think on their feet ... and want to make their feet look good while doing it.

Tress Stress Relief

What's Going On

The homecoming dance is only a week away and you've got serious split ends but no dough to fix them. Don't stress. Haircuts are not the only solution for split ends.

What to Do About It

Grab a few extra-large avocados. Throw away the pit and skin and then mash up what's left until it starts to look like a paste—or really good guacamole. Rub the concoction throughout your dry locks, paying special attention to the ends. You'll want to leave the mixture in your hair for at least 30 minutes. Take this time to surf the Web for a glam hairstyle to sport on the big night. When time is up, wash out the avocado, shampoo like normal, and start looking for a killer dress.

Why It Works

Natural oils in avocado merge the split ends together and keep them glued in place through a few washes. This gives you a chance to postpone that haircut until you have a little extra cash flow.

Sea-son Your Skin to Win

What's Going On

Your flaky, rough skin has left you in need of a full-body exfoliation. But when it comes to deciding between spending your money on a girl's night out or an overpriced scrub, your skin is probably going to lose out.

What to Do About It

Why choose between beauty and fun when you can have both? Get the box of sea salt that has been sitting in the back of the cupboard for years and bring it into the shower. Rub the salt on your body, clean it off, follow with a moisturizer, and head out for girl's night with great skin.

SEA SALT

Why It Works

Salt opens your pores, leaving your skin ready to absorb moisturizer, and sea salt is extra chunky and more crumbly than regular table salt, giving you a softer scrub. The crystals exfoliate your skin, scrubbing off dead cells so the fresh ones below can surface.

on THE Run

Mediterranean Cuticle Cure

You've got shabby cuticles and, unfortunately, there isn't a manicurist on school grounds. But you're not only beautiful, you're resourceful. During your lunch break, ask the cafeteria lady for olive oil in a bowl. Soak your nails in the oil for 15 minutes and then rinse your hands. You'll soften your cuticles, strengthen your nails, and gain a whole new appreciation for the Mediterranean all at the same time.

Tea for Tired Peeps

What's Going On

You've spent the whole night cramming for your chemistry midterm, and it has definitely put a damper on your beauty sleep. You look like a wreck but still need to go to school and take that test.

What to Do About It

Revitalize your sleepy eyes with chamomile: Set two tea bags in a stovetop pot of water and wait for your concoction to boil. Carefully remove the bags and set them in the freezer until thoroughly chilled (this should take at least 10 minutes). Put a bag on each eye and take a power nap. Then, wake up ready to ace the exam.

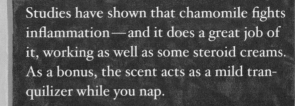

Why It Works

Studies have shown that chamomile fights inflammation—and it does a great job of it, working as well as some steroid creams. As a bonus, the scent acts as a mild tranquilizer while you nap.

15

Mix and Match

Most girls have the usual nail polish colors in their beauty box—red, reddish pink ... and pinkish red. To branch out, pick an eye shadow color you'd like your nail polish to match. Scrape off a small amount of the eye shadow and mix it with clear nail polish on a piece of tin foil. (Mixing the color outside the bottle means you'll be able to keep making new colors.) Test your new hue directly on your nails until you get the perfect shade.

Looking Peachy

What's Going On

You've got yearbook pictures tomorrow. You also have a dry, dull complexion. Your skin needs a quick boost so you can put your best face forward.

What to Do About It

The quest for a glowing complexion can be messy, so throw on an old shirt before you start. Grab an extra-juicy peach and cut a few slices from it. Wash your face and rub these slices all over it, letting the juice sink in. Spend the next 30 minutes contemplating the perfect outfit for your date. When time is up, wash your face thoroughly and check out your new glow.

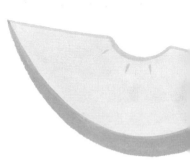

Why It Works

Peaches are naturally stocked with alpha hydroxy acids, which help exfoliate dead skin cells, and vitamins A and C, which are great for the new cells. The juice also unclogs pores to banish blemishes.

Disastrous Dye

What's Going On

That at-home, semi-permanent dye job took a wrong turn somewhere, and now you're stuck with spotty locks.

What to Do About It

Before you drop money on a professional fix or consider wearing a hat until it grows out (which could take a very, very long time), try an at-home repair. It's most effective to fix the color catastrophe within the first 48 hours. To get started, apply a hot-oil treatment (there's a great, cheap recipe in this book on page 42), then wash twice with a dandruff shampoo. The dye should fade, along with the embarrassment.

Why It Works

Semi-permanent dye is meant to wash out eventually. To get it to come out faster than usual, you basically do the opposite of what they suggest to make the dye job last longer. The hot oil loosens the color pigment. Then the dandruff shampoo bonds with the dye and carries it down the drain when you rinse.

21

Short on Makeup Brushes?

The smoky eye shadow you sported last night left its mark on all your makeup brushes. Now it's impossible to use them for the barely there pink look you want today. It's time to tap into your sister's art supplies. Grab a few medium-size paintbrushes (extra clean and free of any actual paint). Use them to apply all of your makeup, from foundation to eye shadow.

Fake Awake

What's Going On

Spending last night with the girls to toilet-paper the neighbor's house was awesome. But now your eyes are shot and you need to look awake when your parents start asking where all the TP went.

What to Do About It

Fake the look of someone who went to bed early last night (instead of sneaking in past 11). Grab some white eye shadow and dab it on the inner corner of your eye. If you still appear drowsy, use the shadow also as a highlighter just under the brow line. (This works on all skin tones.)

Why It Works

The white eye shadow creates an optical illusion that makes your eyes appear more open and bright. Your parents will never know the difference!

Fight Those Stinky Pinkies

What's Going On

You can't believe your luck. The hottest peep-toe shoes are finally on sale, and there's one pair left. You feel like Cinderella, trying on what could be fashion destiny. Well, it may feel like magic—but it sure doesn't smell like it. The odor emanating from your feet is almost unbearable.

What to Do About It

To put an end to the not-so-fairy-tale smell, soak your feet for 30 minutes in a bowl of warm water and three tablespoons of baking soda.

Why It Works

Your chemistry teacher will tell you that if you mix an acid and a base, they react and form water and a salt. Here's why you care: Foot odor is caused by organic acids, and baking soda is a mild base (called sodium bicarbonate). If you mix the two together, you get plain-old water and a salt, neither of which have a smell. Remember, when the odor is away, the peep-toe shoes can come out to play.

On the Go With Scents in Tow

A purse can hold only so much, and you're packin' a lot. Sure, your cell phone, car keys, wallet, and lip gloss are necessities. But with all that squished into your tiny bag, there's no way you're going to fit that bottle of your favorite perfume. To save space, simply spray the perfume on a cotton swab, and place it in a small plastic resealable bag. When you need to reapply your fragrance, just pull out the swab and dab it on.

No Puff Potato

What's Going On

Boyfriend problems have given you an irritating case of insomnia *and* puffy eyes. Before you make up or break up, get your peeps back to normal.

What to Do About It

Expensive gel packs work great on the eyes, but for a fast and cheap solution, potatoes do the trick. Go to the kitchen, and grab a spud and boil it, then remove it from heat. When it becomes just cool enough to the touch, slice it and place the slices on your eyes.

Why It Works

Potatoes contain starch, which works miracles when it comes to reducing redness and puffiness. In addition, the cold causes the capillaries and blood vessels in your skin to narrow, which chills out any dark circles you've picked up in the process. Now you're ready to grab your best friend (not your boyfriend!) for a night out.

No More Loch Ness Monster Locks

What's Going On

After a few laps of the backstroke and a serious game of Marco Polo, you're ready to get back to the fine art of poolside relaxing. There's only one problem holding you back from sun goddess status: Thanks to your dip in the pool, you have seriously gruesome green locks.

What to Do About It

First, casually pull on a hat and head for home. On the way, stop at the store and grab a few cans of tomato juice. Wait for your hair to air-dry. Then get in the shower and rub the tomato juice into your tresses until they are completely soaked in it. Throw on a shower cap (or tie a plastic bag around your hair) and then sit back for 30 minutes and watch your favorite sitcom. When the credits start rolling, hop back in the shower, and wash out the tomato juice. Shampoo and condition your hair as normal. Voilà! The swamp look should be gone!

Why It Works

Your hair turns green because of hard metals (copper, iron, and manganese are the usual culprits) in the pool water. The tomato juice binds with the metals, pulling them from your hair when you rinse.

on THE Run

Oil-Free for Free

Having a hottie as a lab partner is a good thing. The fact that he can see his reflection in your shiny face is not. But when you're at school, you don't always have access to fancy cosmetic blotting papers. Instead, head to the restroom, grab a new toilet seat cover, dab it on your excess oil, and watch the shine disappear.

Vanquish Nasty Nail Stains

What's Going On

After ages of sporting flaming red nail polish, you're ready to give the natural look another go. You remove the ruby paint, only to find icky, stained nails beneath.

What to Do About It

Soak your fingernails in lemon juice for 10 minutes, then gently buff out the stain. Repeat the process each day until your nasty marks are gone.

Why It Works

Lemon juice is a natural astringent and bleach that lifts out the stain your nail polish left behind. Buffing your nails also helps to remove the stained layer—but don't buff too hard, since buffing removes a little nail, too.

Clean Shave

What's Going On
You have a new spring skirt you can't wait to show off. You have also just run out of shaving cream, and hairy legs still aren't in fashion.

What to Do About It
Grab a small bit of shampoo, lather up, shave like normal, and slip on the skirt.

Why It Works
Shaving cream is simply a combination of cleansers and moisturizers. Beauty product manufacturers like us to think it's the only thing to shave with, but it's not. Other beauty products can work just as well. Shampoo is a particularly good option because it foams up nicely, is meant to be used on hairy surfaces, and smells awesome. For extra smoothness after shaving, put a little conditioner on your legs while still in the shower, and rinse.

Visor Advisory

The hours you've spent mastering the perfect updo for the winter formal will mean nothing without plenty of extra-strength hairspray to hold everything in place. But keeping the spray out of your eyes and away from your makeup can be a bit tricky (the shellacked look is not a good thing). Now's the time to use your mom's awful-looking sun visor from the '80s. (If she doesn't have one, check your dad's old poker supplies for the cheesy light-up kind.) Sport the visor look while spraying your locks to keep your hair in place and the sticky stuff off your face.

SPRAY *

Treat Your Tresses

What's Going On

Your hair needs a boost in the shine department, but high-priced, professional hot-oil treatments aren't an option on a student's budget.

What to Do About It

Forget the salon and make an at-home hot-oil treatment for your tresses. Mix two parts canola oil (many households stock it but rarely use it) with one part hot water and apply it to your hair as you would shampoo. Leave the mixture on for five minutes before shampooing out. No more straw!

Why It Works

Everybody's hair needs a little natural oil to stay healthy and shiny. Washing and styling your hair can remove this oil, leaving your hair dull and lifeless. Canola oil is remarkably similar to the oils used in expensive hair treatments. It deep-conditions your hair, adding the gloss you're after.

Towel Tamer for Wet Curls

The rain on the way to school turned your perfectly diffused curls into a perfectly runaway mop. To dry your hair without frizzing out, use the cheap and rough paper towels in the restroom. They are perfect for taking excessive moisture out of curly hair, without causing a fro. Just blot hair with paper towels to soak up the water and head back into the world.

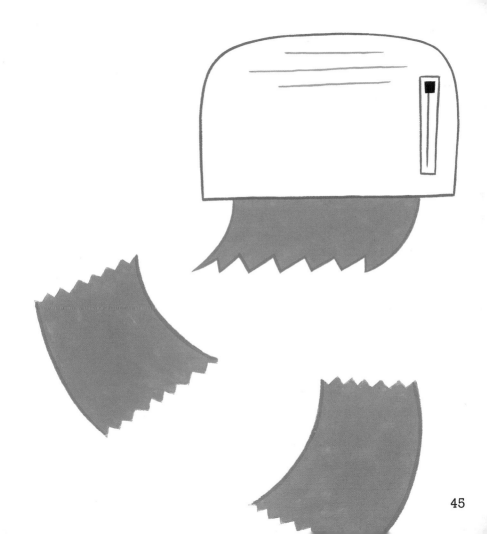

Milk Does the Body Good

What's Going On

Overexerting yourself with prom committee, finals, and the new part-time job—not to mention your social life—has left your skin neglected and in need of some TLC.

What to Do About It

Get your skin baby smooth while taking a bath. As the tub is filling with warm water, add two cups of milk. Soak for 30 minutes, then rinse your body thoroughly.

Why It Works

People have been taking milk baths since Cleopatra's time, but only recently has science figured out why. Milk contains lactic acid, which helps exfoliate your skin, leaving it soft and smooth. You'll feel rejuvenated and ready to conquer one more extracurricular.

Rid the Red

What's Going On

Your birthday happens only once a year. Unfortunately, this one is coinciding with the birth of an enormous zit on your chin.

What to Do About It

Make the pimple look less prominent with the use of over-the-counter eyedrops. As soon as you notice the sucker, saturate a cotton ball with the solution and hold it over the blemish for a few minutes. The redness should fade.

Why It Works

Eyedrops work their magic on bloodshot peepers by shrinking hyperactive blood vessels in your eye. The same reaction will cut the red from inflammation around a zit, leaving you ready to party.

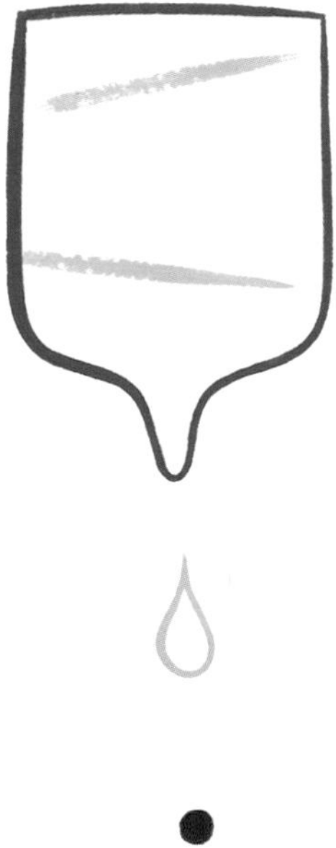

Freeze Those Nails

Before meeting up with your friends, you had just enough time to do your nails. But not enough time to let them dry. It's easy to keep your brand-new manicure in check. While your nails are still wet, run them under very cold water to freeze the paint in place.

Manage Your Mane

What's Going On

You are on your way to a job interview when you realize the humid weather has left your hair in a state of serious distress. The hair-taming products are at home, but your mane is a mess right *now*.

What to Do About It

Before you freak out and cancel the interview, pump a pea-sized amount of body or face lotion into your hands and rub a few drops between your palms. (If you don't have any with you, stop by a store that has free samples.) Then, run your hands through your mane until desired sleekness is achieved.

Why It Works

Despite what the ad campaigns tell you, conditioner is conditioner. Sure, different formulations are better for your hair or your hands, but in a pinch the moisturizers in hand lotion will work their magic on your tresses.

Keep the Dye in Line

You're tired of being overlooked and want a wild new hair color to match your outgoing personality. It's a cool idea—after all, you only live once—but remember that the more extreme the dye color, the worse its remnants will look on your forehead. Before you reach for fire engine red or midnight blue, run lip balm along your hairline to prevent the dye from getting on your skin. Then, go crazy!

lip balm

Cook-Dry Your Nails

What's Going On

You've just finished applying the final touches to your at-home manicure when you realize you have only a few minutes left to dry your nails, put together an outfit, and do your hair before you're late for school.

What to Do About It

Nonstick cooking spray isn't just for making the perfect bacon and eggs. Spray a layer over freshly painted nails to get a faster dry time.

Why It Works

The main chemicals in nail polish are a solid color pigment and a solvent that makes the color pigment turn into a liquid. (All paints work this way.) The chemicals in cooking spray make the solvent evaporate faster, which makes the color harden quicker.

57

Play Hide-the-Hickey

What's Going On

Getting a hickey is fun. Hiding it with a turtleneck in the middle of summer is not. And, your parents are sure to notice if you're wearing wool in 90-degree weather.

What to Do About It

Unfortunately, time is the only complete cure for a hickey. But you can reduce the tell-tale signs of one by doing this little trick. Put a quarter in the freezer until it gets super cold, then press the coin on the hickey for up to 10 minutes. Repeat every two hours.

Why It Works

A hickey is basically a bruise, which is a cluster of broken blood vessels. The cold from the quarter constricts the blood vessels and reduces the swelling in the area. This helps the hickey heal faster. After two days the bruise should lighten up enough so that the old "I burned myself with the curling iron" excuse just might work.

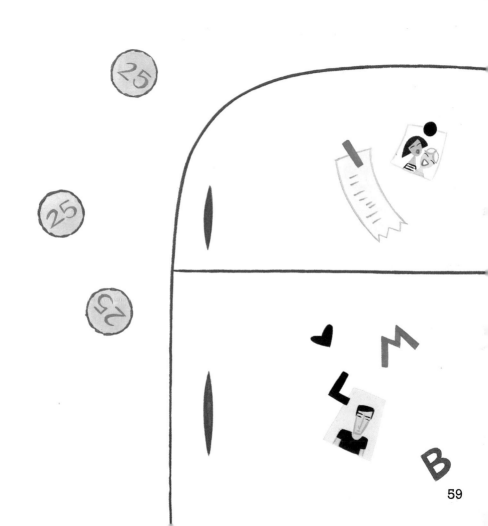

Make the Most of Eye Makeup

Finding yourself low on eyeliner and equally low on funds to buy more? No need to rob a bank. With one easy step, eye shadow can be made into eyeliner. Just grab an angled makeup brush to apply a thin line of eye shadow in place of the liner. For a liquid liner look, wet the angled brush before dipping it in the shadow.

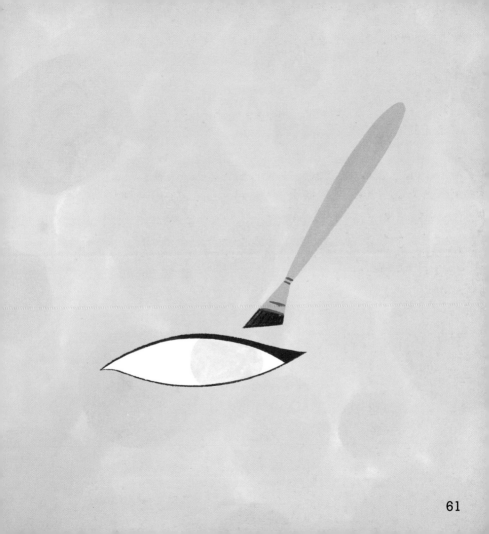

Juice Up Your Highlights

What's Going On

You scored the super-cute bikini (on sale) and the designer shades (thrift store find), but the salon-style streaks just don't fit into your seashore budget.

What to Do About It

If you already have blond or light-brown hair, you can simply hit the beach to achieve summertime locks for free. Lemons (in combination with sunlight and heat) can give a natural boost of color to your hair. Juice 5 to 10 lemons—depending on the length of your mane—and pour the juice into a clean spray bottle. When the sun is out, spray your hair from roots to ends and comb through. Lay out (with sunscreen, of course) and let the juice do its thing.

Why It Works

When lemon juice combines with sunlight, it acts as a natural bleach. Be sure to do this on a sunny day, though—lemon juice without sunlight gives you a fresh scent but no highlights.

Volumize on a Bathroom Break

You woke up early and did your 'do before school. You hoped your put-together hair would help you look pulled together for your big presentation in second period. Unfortunately, by the time you made it to class, your mane had lost its volume and you'd lost your confidence.

No need to catch the next bus home. Head to the nearest bathroom for a quick touch-up. Place your hair under a hand dryer. The hot air will add extra charge to the styling products you used that morning.

Hot Lashes

What's Going On

You've been using an eyelash curler since before you were even allowed to wear mascara. Now, you think your everyday curly lashes have started to look just plain normal. You want extra oomph.

What to Do About It

The tool isn't the problem—the way you use it is. Try running your regular curler under hot (but still touchable) water for 10 to 15 seconds before using it to get an even bigger, more eye-catching curl.

Why It Works

The warm water gives you enough heat to get those lashes in line the same way a curling iron does for longer hair, but without the risk of burning yourself.

Quick Shave

What's Going On

Your date is waiting downstairs, but a last-minute mirror check reveals a nasty case of leg stubble. And there's no time to hop back in the shower. Like you weren't nervous enough. Now you're going to spend the night wondering if he's noticed the bristles.

What to Do About It

Play it cool and tell him you'll be right down (you're worth waiting for). Next, rub a good amount of baby oil on your legs and take the razor to them.

Why It Works

The baby oil acts as a protective barrier between the blades and your skin, minimizing the nicks and razor burn. You'll get a quick, smooth shave and have an even smoother date.

69

Eyelash Spark From a Spork

You're sitting in the lunchroom and thinking about next period: calculus. It's hard not to like a class overflowing with guys who have both brawn *and* brains. You want to look your best, but you've got only a few minutes, in between chowing down and socializing, to add some zing to your appearance.

The plastic spork comes to the rescue. These spoon-fork hybrids aren't just for eating mystery meat—they can also help you get extra curly (and flirty) lashes. First, grab a mirror and close the first eye you want to start on. Next, press the rounded back part of the utensil under your top lashes and roll toward the ceiling (keep pressing!) until you achieve desired curliness.

Makeup Matchup

What's Going On

As a fashionable woman, you hold color coordination in the highest regard. The purse must match the shoes, and the polish on your hands and feet should always be painted from the same bottle. And when it comes to lip gloss? You change your eye shadow so often that, if you bought a new lip color each time, you'd go broke trying to keep up.

What to Do About It

Luckily, you can create your own lip tint. Once you've found the eye shadow color you'd like to mimic in a gloss, take a small piece of the shadow and mix with an even smaller dab of petroleum jelly. Experiment with different proportions of eye shadow and jelly until you get the perfect shade.

Why It Works

Most lip glosses are made up of color pigments suspended in a shiny gel-like petroleum jelly. When you mix the two together, the color stays put in the gel and on your lips.

+

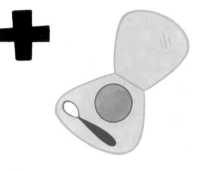

=

Over Easy Locks

What's Going On

A good-looking DMV photo is a must because it's the one pic that's going to have to represent you for the next few years. When photo day is near, give your locks a needed tune-up.

What to Do About It

Your hair needs extra conditioning in preparation for the big day. Crack an egg into a bowl (leave the shell out), and whisk until you have what looks like the start to a perfect omelet. Brush the mixture on your hair, leave on for five minutes, and then wash like normal.

Why It Works

Any nutritionist will tell you that eggs are full of protein and fat. Turns out that these are the perfect ingredients for nourishing your tresses. The nutrients soak into the hair shafts, giving your hair that perfect softness you need for a model-worthy pic.

Erase That Stain

Even if you've got perfect hair, a rockin' manicure, and an unbeatable brain to match, no one is going to notice if underarm deodorant marks are stealing the show (gross—but at least you're using a deodorant, right?). To combat unsightly white marks on the run, hit the nearest bathroom stall and remove one of your socks. Turn the sock inside out (hopefully you washed your feet this morning) and vigorously rub the stain until it disappears.

Forget Flakes

What's Going On

It's hard to pull off the bohemian poet/coffeehouse-regular look when your dandruff is holding you back from wearing black.

What to Do About It

Try using apple cider vinegar. Put two tablespoons of the liquid in a spray bottle and spritz the entire mixture on your scalp. Depending on how bad your 'druff is, let the vinegar remain on from 15 minutes to three hours. Take a shower to shampoo it out.

Why It Works

Dandruff is often caused by clogged pores and a high pH level on your scalp, which can be the result of using lots of hair products. The vinegar balances the pH level and helps clear pores. This keeps the shoulder snow at bay and brings your black sweaters back into circulation.

Tough-Top Tip

What's Going On

Sifting through your collection of nail polish to find just the right color is definitely a challenge. But even after you find that color, the battle's not over—now you have to get the top off the bottle. If it hasn't been opened in years, you could be in for quite a workout.

What to Do About It

To prevent future struggles, rub petroleum jelly around the inside of the nail polish top, where it meets and turns around the bottle. Do this every few uses.

Why It Works

Petroleum jelly is a known lubricant used for all kinds of things (like getting a too-small ring off your finger). It keeps your nail polish from gluing the bottle shut and takes the muscle work out of your manicure.

Greasy Hair Meets Its Match

Your friends keep asking why your hair is wet—when it's not raining and you didn't just take a shower. It's grease, and it's gross, but it won't have you in its grip for long. For light-colored but oily tresses, sprinkle a very small amount of baby powder on the roots and rub it in. If the hair looks too white, you've put too much powder on and you'll need to shake out the excess or make a different part in your hair. If you've got dark hair, dip a cotton ball in witch hazel and dab it on the greasy area. When friends ask what's different about you, tell them you took the time to dry your hair this morning.

Banish Blackheads

What's Going On

First impressions are everything, especially when you've finally secured a date with your crush. Unfortunately, your unsightly blackheads won't help to impress.

What to Do About It

Tomatoes aren't just for salads and burgers. Grab one, cut it in half, and rub the juicy part on your face. Let it soak into your skin for at least 10 minutes, then wash it off with water. Repeat this process every day.

Why It Works

The acidic traits of tomatoes help thoroughly clean the skin and clear the clogged pores that become blackheads. Soon, you'll notice your blackheads disappearing—and your first date begging for a second.

Subdue the Stink

What's Going On

Last night's camping trip was awesome—you got to catch up with your best buds and relive your Girl Scout days. This morning, however, your mane has a fire pit stink and you have an important college interview.

What to Do About It

A good shower is obviously the best way to get the stink out, but when there's no time to wash, grab a dryer sheet from the laundry room. Rub your locks from roots to ends for a fresh, just-cleaned smell.

Why It Works

Fabric softener sheets work in the dryer by coating your clothes with a fragrance that makes them smell good. Rubbing your hair with the sheet transfers the fragrance to your smelly strands.

Stay-in-Place Lemon-Fresh Locks

Out of hairspray and short on time to go get more? Add one sliced lemon to a pot of two cups of water and boil. After it has cooled, place the mixture in a spray bottle and start taming that mane.

Espresso Glow

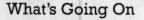

What's Going On

You're at a new school, and after a week of meeting new people, dabbling in new makeup, and just plain trying to make a good impression, your skin is feeling pretty ... blah.

What to Do About It

Perk up with a coffee facial. Ask your mom or dad to give you the coffee grounds after they brew a pot. Let the grounds cool and mix a quarter cup with one egg white. Massage the mixture onto your face, and wait for it to dry. Rinse with warm water to reveal a gently exfoliated complexion.

Why It Works

The coffee grounds work as a scrub and slough off old cells while supplying antioxidants to your skin. The egg white base, as it dries, forms a sort of mask that, when peeled away, removes impurities in your skin. The result: smoother, rejuvenated skin.

A Sticky Situation

When your best friend first started blowing bubbles from a huge wad of chewing gum, it seemed funny enough. When the pink glob became one with your hair, you stopped laughing. Before you shave your head and join the army, try massaging some vegetable oil into the sticky mess. This should make the gum soft and easy to gently pull out.

Sock It to Dry Feet

What's Going On

After a day of marathon shopping, you're thrilled about the perfect outfit you pulled together at half the price. Your feet, however, are not so thrilled—they're tired, dry, and in need of some pampering.

What to Do About It

Rub a good moisturizer into your aching feet and slide them into socks filled with a little baby powder. Keep the socks on overnight.

Why It Works

Wearing socks helps to keep the moisturizer on your feet instead of evaporating or rubbing off onto your blankets, while the baby powder keeps your socks from soaking up all the moisturizer. The next morning, after a thorough moisturizing, your feet will be smooth, relaxed, and ready to hit another round of sales.

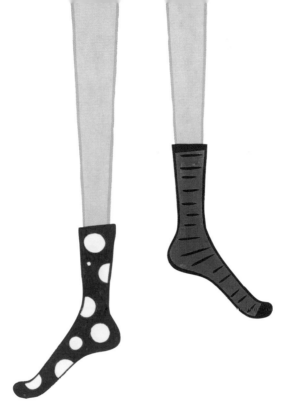

About the Contributors

 **Somer Flaherty** lives in San Francisco, California. She is an editor at *Marin Magazine*, a freelance writer, and a former editor for the national teen newsmagazine *Loud*. When not writing she likes to people-watch and test wacky beauty tips on her friends.

 **Jen Kollmer** is a San Francisco-based freelance writer, a filmmaker, and a former engineer. Her dramatic works have been published in *Fourteen Hills* journal and staged at the Kennedy Center and in the Marin Headlands. She also coauthored Zest Books' *Girl in a Funk: Quick Stress Busters (and why they work)*.

 **Ali Douglass** is a San Francisco-based freelance illustrator. Her work has been featured in advertisements, greeting cards, and apparel, and in publications such as *The NY Times*, *YM*, and *Seventeen*.